The story of the world's last sea-going paddle steamer

Eighth Edition – June 2001
Published by Waverley Excursions Ltd., Anderston Quay, Glasgow, G3 8HA.

ISBN 0 9505177 7 1

Compiled and designed by Fraser MacHaffie, Joe McKendrick and Leslie Brown

Photographs are by the authors or are reproduced by courtesy of Messrs. Eric Armstrong, Julian Bowden-Green, R. B. Boyd, Stuart Cameron, Richard Danielson, John Goss, The Herald, Michael Hupton, Graham E. Langmuir, Ian McCorkindale, Douglas McGowan, James Moore, Derek Peters, Iain Quinn, Gordon Reid, G. Rickwood, Robert Scott, Ian H. Shannon, Leo J. Vogt and Edwin Wilmshurst.

WELCOME ABOARD!

It's difficult to believe that, for almost half her life, *Waverley* has sailed under the houseflag of her own company – Waverley Steam Navigation Company Limited.

Raised from comparative obscurity, *Waverley* has now been seen and enjoyed around the entire British coast. Built to sail between Craigendoran and Arrochar, *Waverley* has now sailed right round Britain, crossed to Northern Ireland and Eire, and come to within hailing distance of the French coast.

Those of us who work with *Waverley*, whether ashore or afloat, are confident this ship has a future and can continue to give pleasure to hundreds of thousands each year. This confidence is shown in the major investment programmes over the years, culminating in the recent major rebuild. Much of the passenger accommodation has been refurbished with the aim of making her more comfortable while retaining as far as possible the original charm, character and appearance of the whole vessel.

This booklet tells something of *Waverley's* history, her journeying and the work that goes on to keep alive an irreplaceable part of the nation's maritime heritage. On board *Waverley* you can actually see the massive steam engine at work, watch the paddles push us through the water, walk on wooden decks, smell that unique steamboat smell and enjoy the fresh sea breezes.

By your support and interest you can help write the story of *Waverley's* future.

Enjoy your sail with us. We trust it will not be long before we welcome you on board again.

Graeme Gellatly,
Master, P.S. *Waverley*
June 2001

WAVERLEY GOES TO WAR

In time of war, the Clyde steamers have played a vital rôle in the defence of this country. An earlier *Waverley* saw service in both World Wars and is shown above in April 1940 off the south coast of England in the company of the Caledonian Steam Packet's *Duchess of Fife*. The *Fife* returned to the Clyde but *Waverley* paid the supreme sacrifice on 29 May 1940 when returning with troops from the Dunkirk beaches. (In passing, it is interesting to record that the remains of *Waverley* were found by a Belgian diver in the summer of 1985 and a few artifacts salvaged before leaving her in peace again.)

The London and North Eastern Railway lost two ships during the hostilities – *Waverley* and another paddle steamer *Marmion*. Plans to replace both were drawn up but only one ship was to be built. This was the present *Waverley*, and the order went to A. & J. Inglis, Ltd. In 1866 this yard had built the first two Clyde steamers for the North British Railway and eighty years later work started on the last paddler for the LNER, successor to the NB, and the last for the Clyde.

In all, the Inglis yard at Pointhouse, Glasgow, turned out eleven ships for the north bank services from Helensburgh and Craigendoran. The yard's final contribution to the Clyde steamer fleet came in 1953 when the motorships *Maid of Argyll* and *Maid of Skelmorlie* joined the CSP fleet. Inglis also constructed the last paddle steamer to be built for passenger traffic in the British Isles – Loch Lomond's *Maid of the Loch*.

The 1899 Waverley *in her peacetime days, when she ranked among the fastest of the Clyde steamers.*

A. & J. Inglis undertook the conversion back to civilian service of the two LNER paddlers that survived active duty – the impressive *Jeanie Deans* dating from 1931, and the unique and perpetually-shaking *Talisman*, a diesel-electric paddler built by Inglis in 1935. The reconstruction produced ships considerably altered from their 1939 layout and appearance and the new paddler's plans closely resembled the general scheme of the rehabilitated *Jeanie*.

A misty 2nd October, 1946, saw the last paddle steamer to be built for the Clyde services named by Lady Matthews, wife of the LNER Chairman.
The choice of the name *Waverley* perpetuated the memory of the North British flier of 1899 and a suitable plaque was placed on the new ship. The north bank steamers were traditionally named after the novels or characters from the works of Sir Walter Scott.

Right: The Victoria Harbour, Greenock in February 1947.

The new *Waverley* was a shade smaller than the 1931 *Jeanie*. Her length, for example, at 240' was 11' less and her passenger certificate allowed 1,350 as against 1,480. First and second class accommodation was provided including a dining saloon, lounge, tearoom and shop on the main deck with a bar and tearoom on the lower deck. Two large deck shelters were constructed on the promenade deck with the bridge, wheelhouse, master's room and two lifeboats placed over the forward shelter. Passengers shared the deck above the after shelter with two lifeboats and the mainmast.

The engine in Rankin & Blackmore's Eagle Foundry in Greenock.

Once the fitting out of *Waverley* was well advanced, the new steamer was towed from Pointhouse to Greenock's Victoria Harbour where Rankin & Blackmore fitted the double-ended boiler and the magnificent triple-expansion steam engine. She was fitted with 18-ft diameter rimless paddle wheels each with eight flat wooden feathering floats. For her first ten years, she was coal-fired but in 1957 her boiler was converted to burn heavy fuel oil.

Waverley on trials in June 1947 when a top speed of 18·5 knots was attained with the engine running at 56 rpm. In service 15 knots is usually adequate but a reserve is there if the need arises.

The LNER eschewed the CSP practice of the 1930s of disguising the paddle boxes of their steamers and *Waverley* carries a fan-vented paddle box of traditional appearance with scroll work and figurehead of Scott's hero, Edward Waverley.

In 1947, *Waverley* was one of a multitude of steamers fitted with triple expansion engines. Now, she is alone in her class. The experience of gazing on the three massive pistons and cranks as they silently and effortlessly propel the vessel is reserved today for only those on board *Waverley*.

WAVERLEY IN HER ELEMENT

Left: Crossing Rothesay Bay during the summer of 1947.

Below: Waverley's *paddlebox on her first day in service*

The new paddle steamer was to take her share of the ferry work from Craigendoran to the Clyde Coast resorts but *Waverley's* maiden voyage on Monday, 16th June, 1947 was on the route for which she was primarily intended – the cruise up Loch Goil and Loch Long to the villages of Lochgoilhead and Arrochar. The sailing was part of the popular Three Lochs Tour which allowed the traveller to enjoy a circular tour including a sail on one of the Loch Lomond paddlers from Balloch at the south end to Tarbet.

From Tarbet the excursionist crossed, on foot or by coach, the narrow strip of land separating the freshwater Loch Lomond from the sealoch Loch Long. At Arrochar, *Waverley* was joined to complete another part of the circle via Loch Long and Loch Goil. Lochgoilhead Pier was the link in two circular tours available in certain years to passengers on *Waverley*. A coach left Lochgoilhead for Inveraray going via Rest-and-be-Thankful. One of the swift turbine steamers, usually *Duchess of Montrose*, was boarded at Inveraray for the return leg of the journey. Another possibility was to travel by coach from Dunoon via Loch Eck and Hell's Glen to Lochgoilhead where *Waverley* would be waiting.

Waverley sailed to Arrochar six times a week in 1947 but in the last year Arrochar Pier was in use, 1972, the frequency had dropped to once weekly. In July 1965 Lochgoilhead Pier was closed, having been declared unsafe, and soon thereafter dismantled.

Captain John Cameron *(right)* and Chief Engineer William Summers joined *Waverley* in 1947. Captain Cameron left *Waverley* in 1948 and Captain Donald Crawford took command for a time.

Bill Summers remained with *Waverley* until retirement came in 1969. When Waverley S.N.Co. took over the paddler in 1974, it was clear that *Waverley* had become more than a job to Bill who welcomed the chance to get close again to his engines and he made his years of experience available to the new owners. His contribution was significant during those early difficult years. Bill Summers passed away in 1977 and John Cameron eleven years later, but their enthusiasm for the ship's preservation is acknowledged by plaques on board.

CHANGE — FOR THE BETTER?

The arrival of a camera in the Spring of 1948 at Bowling Harbour captures the disappearance of the LNER funnel colours.

Waverley was allowed only one season to sail in the attractive LNER colours. Her hull and paddle boxes were black while the former carried two gold lines immediately beneath the cream topsides. The deck shelters were grained brown. Above towered red funnels with black tops and white bands.

At the end of 1947 the various privately-owned railway companies were grouped into a nationalised British Transport Commission and the need for uniformity rode roughshod over aesthetic considerations. The bright funnel colours were painted over with the drab buff and black of the BTC. The Clyde would wait a quarter of a century before once again seeing the red, white and black.

In November 1951 the Craigendoran paddlers – *Jeanie Deans*, *Talisman* and *Waverley* – were transferred to the Commission's Scottish shipping subsidiary, The Caledonian Steam Packet Co. Ltd. This allowed the eventual replacement of the buff by more-pleasing Caley bright yellow.

The 1951 change in ownership affected each of the ships differently. The *Jeanie* saw minimal change and was seldom asked to carry out tasks alien to a "north bank" steamer. *Talisman*, on the other hand, was re-engined within three years and became the regular steamer in summer on the Caledonian Wemyss Bay-Largs-Millport-Kilchattan Bay service.

The integration of *Waverley* into the CSP fleet was gradual and she saw increasing service on the ferry routes from Gourock and Wemyss Bay. Her cruising programme in summer was widened at the expense of Arrochar trips. In 1953, *Waverley* began a Monday sailing from Craigendoran through the Kyles of Bute to Brodick, Lamlash and Whiting Bay. This excursion remained with her until 1971. Lamlash Pier was closed at the end of 1954 and Whiting Bay went likewise in 1961 and *Waverley* latterly called at Brodick and then sailed towards Pladda at the south end of Arran.

In 1955 *Waverley* revived an excursion with Caledonian origins when she sailed "Round the Lochs" on Wednesdays. Three years later our steamer fell heir to a day-trip introduced in 1957 by the turbine *Marchioness of Graham*. This was the "Up-River" sailing from Largs, Rothesay and Dunoon to Glasgow. The *Graham* had been sold out of the fleet and so Friday visits to Glasgow (Bridge Wharf) became a regular feature of *Waverley's* summer programme.

Waverley now even deputised occasionally on the turbine steamer cruises from Gourock and Glasgow. From 1958 to 1962 she took the Gourock cruises of *Duchess of Hamilton* for the closing weeks of the season. Alan Brown in his book "Craigendoran Steamers" recalls:

"*Waverley* probably reached her peak in the late 'fifties when, under the command of Captain Colin Mackay and with Bill Summers at the throttle, she achieved an enviable reputation for punctuality and general smartness. Friday, 26th September, 1958 was an outstanding day in *Waverley's* career, for on that day she was rostered for the first time to take the Gourock-Ayr sailing, with its associated cruise round Holy Isle. She had deputised for *Duchess of Hamilton* the whole of that week and it was obvious that the Mackay/Summers team was determined to put up a good show on the exacting long cruises.

"Throughout the week *Waverley* had maintained excellent timings, and great interest centred on the Ayr run, for it was on this that she faced her stiffest task. It was therefore with considerable anticipation and excitement that I made my way down to Gourock Pier that calm, crisp, sunny autumn morning; nor was I disappointed, for *Waverley* gave me the most enjoyable and thrilling sail I have had on the Clyde in post-war days. The whole day was tightly scheduled, but nevertheless she arrived at Ayr in ample time to commence her afternoon cruise round Holy Isle at 1.45pm. Leaving Ayr one minute late on the return run to Gourock she pounded homewards, her triple cranks spinning round at an effortless 50 rpm and her wooden floats endlessly repeating their intoxicating 'eight beats to the bar' rhythm.

Right: Waverley *at Dunoon in BTC colours*

"Slicing through the dark, glassy water, she left a broad carpet of foam trailing astern, and as she curved round into Gourock there was a general air of triumph on board. Alongside the pier *Duchess of Hamilton* lay at peace, and on the after deck a number of her crew were seated, perhaps speculating on the hour of *Waverley's* return. The look of utter astonishment and blank disbelief on their faces as *Waverley* berthed, three minutes ahead of schedule, still remains as a vivid memory of September 26th, 1958."

Waverley passing Queen's Dock, Glasgow, in July 1959, showing the white paddleboxes and old funnels. Although it is difficult to recognise it, this is now the site of the Scottish Exhibition and Conference Centre.

Waverley on Saturday 20th September 1958. She is making a fast stop at Lochranza while on the return leg of the Gourock-Campbeltown cruise.

If Alan Brown is correct and *Waverley* was at her peak in the late fifties, she quickly fell into a trough in the early sixties. The standard of day-to-day maintenance dropped and the ship presented a very down-at-heel appearance. Colin MacKay had retired early in 1960 and a less steady hand was at the helm. After some years of neglect *Waverley's* fortunes took a turn for the better and more energetic hands took control.

During the 1950s and 1960s attrition in the CSP passenger fleet brought new summer duties to *Waverley*. As already mentioned, *Waverley* took over the Up-river cruise in 1958 and Saturdays in the same year found her on Wemyss Bay-Rothesay ferry duty. The Caley paddler *Jupiter* had been withdrawn at the end of the previous summer and the motorship *Maid of Skelmorlie* had picked up most of the paddler's duties. Traffic at Wemyss Bay on Saturdays, however, required a passenger capacity greater than the *Maid's* 625, and the Craigendoran paddler shuttled to and fro while the *Maid* sailed on the quieter run between Craigendoran and Rothesay.

Waverley *leaving Wemyss Bay.*

Starting in the 1961 summer, *Waverley* and her older sister *Jeanie Deans* began alternating on the Craigendoran excursions. This meant *Waverley* spent every other week on the afternoon Round Bute cruise. *Jeanie Deans* had been in decline for many years but towards the end of her Clyde career a change in personnel and duties put some pep back into the old girl and there were some hotly-contested sprints as both paddlers headed home in the evening.

Jeanie Deans was withdrawn at the end of September 1964 and the next season found the paddle steamer *Caledonia* at Craigendoran with *Waverley*. The two paddlers alternated on the Wednesday Round the Lochs but otherwise tended to perform the same duties each week with *Waverley* sailing Round Bute on Monday, to Arrochar on Tuesday and Thursday, and Up-river to Glasgow on Friday. On Saturday and Sunday both steamers operated from Craigendoran.

Below: The two paddlers Caledonia *and* Waverley *at Craigendoran in August 1965.*

Waverley's former stablemate, *Talisman*, shook her last late in 1966. The next summer, *Waverley's* Sunday duties were recast to include *Talisman's* popular afternoon sailing from Millport and Largs to Rothesay and Tighnabruaich. This arrangement held for the next two seasons also.

COLOUR SCHEMES

Change in ownership forced *Waverley* to abandon the LNER livery in early 1948. The British Transport Commission's funnel colours of dull buff and black tops were adopted.

The Craigendoran fleet in BTC days with (left to right) Talisman, Lucy Ashton, Jeanie Deans *and* Waverley *catching the evening sun. The North British Railway opened Craigendoran pier in May 1882 and it remained the "north bank" terminal until its closure by the Scottish Transport Group at the end of the 1972 summer.*

The Caledonian Steam Packet's imprint was seen in 1953 when the deck saloons were painted white and the ventilators, previously grained, were now silver with blue interiors. The paddle boxes of *Waverley* became white in late May 1959.

In common with the other CSP cruise vessels, radar was fitted before the 1960 summer. Metal corrosion caused the replacement of *Waverley's* funnels in two stages: the forward funnel in 1961 and the after in 1962. The new ones, which were welded rather than riveted, were much heavier than their predecessors, and the extra weight caused a slight sag in the deck resulting in the funnels being marginally out of alignment.

Waverley *approaching Keppel, Cumbrae's second pier for many years, on a June evening in 1963 while on the Round the Lochs cruise.*

By 1972, *Waverley* was the sole surviving Clyde paddler and to accentuate her uniqueness, the paddle boxes were painted black. A new flag and funnel colouring in 1973 reflected the union of the Caledonian S. P. Co. with much of David MacBrayne Ltd. into Caledonian MacBrayne Ltd. Funnels were red with black tops (MacBrayne) and bore yellow discs with red lions (Caledonian).

British Rail introduced a new colour scheme for their fleets in 1965 and this was adopted in part by the railway-owned Clyde steamers. The hulls were painted blue while deck railings and ventilators became grey. Instead of the BR red funnel, rather small red Caledonian lions rampant were fitted to the yellow funnels *(above)*. In January 1969, the CSP became a subsidiary of the Scottish Transport Group and after that summer the hulls reverted to black.

THE END OF AN ERA?

Waverley's regular routine in the summer of 1973 included the Round Bute sail on Sundays, Mondays and Thursdays – from Gourock though, not Craigendoran which was closed after the 1972 summer season. On Tuesdays and Wednesdays she gave the Round the Lochs day cruise while on Fridays Tarbert was the destination. Saturdays were spent on ferry work in the morning with an afternoon cruise to Tighnabruaich. *Waverley* gave a number of Showboat Evening Cruises from Largs and Rothesay to the Kyles of Bute. On Mondays from 28th May to 9th July further variety was introduced when *Waverley* was allocated the morning commuter run from Brodick to Ardrossan since no other vessel was available.

As the 1973 season drew to a close, clearly *Waverley's* future was in question and two enthusiasts' groups arranged special sailings. The Clyde River Steamer Club had the ship on Saturday 15th September and called at Brodick and Campbeltown. Two weeks later, the Paddle Steamer Preservation Society took her on a Five Lochs cruise *(left)* visiting the Holy Loch plus Lochs Riddon, Striven, Long and Goil. *Waverley's* last day in service for Caledonian MacBrayne, Sunday 30th September, was spent being filmed in the morning and later sailing round Bute. On 1st October, she entered James Watt Dock, Greenock, for lay-up.

Waverley's track record in 1973 had not been good. Nine days' sailings had been cancelled because of mechanical trouble and her schedule had been interrupted on many other occasions. The motor ship *Maid of Argyll* had been available to cover for both *Waverley* and *Queen Mary II* but the *Argyll* was now on the Sale List and would leave for the Mediterranean in April 1974.

The results of the 1973 cruising programme were described in the Scottish Transport Group's annual report as "particularly disappointing" (even though *Waverley* carried more passengers in 1973 than in any of the preceding ten years). The prospect of operating two ageing, unreliable and expensive cruise ships on the Clyde was too much for the STG and the 1974 Clyde excursion programme was to be curtailed to a single ship – *Queen Mary II*. The STG report continues, "As a result of this decision, the PS *Waverley* has been taken out of service and, as the last sea-going paddler, has been offered for preservation".

SOLD FOR A POUND

Perhaps today a pound can't buy much but in August 1974 it bought a 693-ton paddle steamer! The Scottish Transport Group recognised that the withdrawal of *Waverley* marked the end of an era stretching from 1812 when Henry Bell's little paddler *Comet* sailed from Glasgow. The Paddle Steamer Preservation Society had been actively interested in *Waverley* for a number of years. The two organisations came together in November 1973 and, through Caledonian MacBrayne, the STG offered the vessel to the PSPS. At that time there was no thought of returning the steamer to service, rather she was to become a static restaurant/museum operation.

The pound that bought Waverley.
Left to right: Terry Sylvester and Douglas McGowan (WSN), Sir Patrick Thomas (STG) and John Whittle (CalMac).

But a static, silent steamer is a poor substitute for a vibrant, moving, alive paddler. By the end of 1973, Terry Sylvester and Douglas McGowan, two active and optimistic members of the PSPS, were investigating ways of returning *Waverley* to service and within a few months the local authorities were approached with a novel idea. The last sea-going paddle steamer could be a tourist attraction for the south west region of Scotland. The City of Glasgow, Strathclyde Region and others were invited to join in the experiment of running a paddle steamer.

On 8th August 1974, *Waverley* was officially handed over by CalMac to Waverley Steam Navigation Company Ltd., a company formed by the PSPS. The price tag was one pound and was satisfied by a donation from Sir Patrick Thomas, chairman of the STG.

That was the easy part. *Waverley* lay idle in the James Watt Dock while her fate was debated in council chambers around the country. But the enthusiasts were not idle. Recognising the "put up or shut up" challenge from the STG, PSPS members and friends formed working parties and set about cleaning up the ship and ticking off items on a long maintenance list.

The marketing of *Waverley* as a Scottish asset began right away and the funnels were returned to their pristine red, white and black. This allowed a public appeal to be launched for funds to add to an anonymous gift of £10,000 and £11,000 from Glasgow Corporation.

Returning the funnels to black, white and red. The Caledonian lions have been removed, and there has been a first attempt at marking the white/red boundary. The depth of the white band was insufficient and was shortly to be increased.

If *Waverley* was to sail in the summer of 1975 she had to be drydocked for survey and major repairs. No word had come from the newly-formed Strathclyde Region about the funds essential for *Waverley's* future. Waverley S.N.Co. took a gamble (not to be the last!) and booked their steamer into Scott's Garvel Drydock on 17th February 1975 for a four-week stay.

During the drydocking the welcome announcement came of a £30,000 grant from Strathclyde Region. *Waverley* would sail again. Harrisons (Clyde) were appointed as the ship's technical managers and this added credibility to the venture at a time sceptics were not hard to find.

By April 1975, officers and crew were being engaged including Captain David L. Neill who came from Western Ferries' *Sound of Sanda*. The public appeal had raised over £40,000 and the Scottish Tourist Board added £30,000.

The fires were lit on 10th May 1975 and five days later *Waverley* moved out of dock for trials.

Waverley leaves Anderston Quay on her first cruise on 22nd May 1975.

After an extremely busy seven days, the City of Glasgow Police Pipe Band gave *Waverley* a magnificent send off for her first passenger sailing on Thursday 22nd May 1975. All who had helped in some way return to *Waverley* to service were on board for the sail from Glasgow to Dunoon.

Waverley approaches Dunoon with Queen Mary II *alongside*.

Five weeks of charter and public sailings followed before *Waverley* took up her regular summer timetable. With unusual prescience, the STG had included a "non-competitive" clause in the Sale Agreement. This forced *Waverley* into cruising territory abandoned years before by the nationalised body as uneconomic. In July and August 1975, *Waverley* was based for four days each week at the busy commercial port of Ayr and at Glasgow three days.

Day excursions were offered and in addition to calls at the usual piers, the timetable included Troon, Greenock and Kilcreggan.

(It was 1979 before dredging opened up Helensburgh Pier for regular calls by *Waverley*). The return of *Waverley* in 1975 meant that Clyde cruising had become a possibility again for a large section of the population and visitors in south-west Scotland.

The ingenuity of the WSN timetable, the effectiveness of the publicity and the excellent summer weather combined to produce several days when passengers had to be turned away. Even though boiler trouble occasionally disrupted sailings, *Waverley* carried over 121,000 excursionists before the season ended on Monday 8th

Waverley in the colours of Waverley Steam Navigation Co. Ltd. This approximated to her original arrangement, though the deck houses remained white and the brown and gold lining on the hull was not attempted. Also, the outer rim and base of the paddle box were white.

Here we see *Waverley* backing out of Tarbert.

A busy day at Glasgow, Friday June 24th, 1977. Waverley awaits her passengers for Dunoon and Loch Goil. Glen Sannox, far right, arrives to take over from Queen Mary, disabled with boiler trouble.

September and *Waverley* laid up at Glasgow for the winter. By the end of the 1975 summer it was recognised that *Waverley* could be more than a nine-day wonder. Many had assumed the venture would fold sometime in June with money, energy, patience and credit exhausted, but the ship and those involved persevered and the possibility was seen of *Waverley* having a long term future in Clyde cruising.

But financial hurdles remained. Strathclyde Regional Council decided against any financial support for *Waverley* in 1976 despite a strong recommendation from consultants hired by them to investigate Clyde cruising as part of the Region's tourist industry. The Regional Council put its money behind Caledonian MacBrayne – first *Queen Mary* and later *Glen Sannox*. The turbine *Mary* lasted two more seasons before being withdrawn.

As we know, *Waverley* survived, thanks to help from various District Councils – Glasgow being foremost among them – the Scottish Tourist Board and many, many individuals.

Part of the deal struck between CalMac and Strathclyde Region in the Spring of 1976 required the return of *Queen Mary* to Glasgow on three days a week, putting the two ships in direct competition. A compromise was reached but on Sunday mornings that summer both the turbine and the paddler sailed from Glasgow – the first time since 1951 that two steamers had sailed regularly from Glasgow. *Waverley's* 1976 season was very successful with the ship being continuously in steam from 10 May to 22 September and passenger carryings up 50 per cent – even with the Glasgow trade being shared with *Queen Mary*.

The Region's administrators favoured *Queen Mary* and *Glen Sannox* but the aficionado and the general public voted with their feet for *Waverley!* CalMac again abandoned Glasgow at the end of the 1979 season. *Waverley* sailed from Glasgow one day the following year with a broom (for clean sweeping!) at her masthead. The car ferry/cruise ship *Glen Sannox's* involvement in cruising slowly dwindled. In late 1980 CalMac announced the abandonment of all Clyde cruising, but later seasons have found ferries such as *Glen Sannox, Jupiter* and *Keppel* on trips on the upper firth.

FURTH OF THE FIRTH

The short season has always been a problem for the Clyde excursion steamers. In 1976, *Waverley* was in service for about eighteen weeks and in that time had to earn enough to keep her for a whole year.

An exciting opportunity to extend the 1977 season came to WSN late in 1976. Llandudno Pier was to celebrate its centenary in May 1977 and Aberconwy Council offered to sponsor a visit by *Waverley* to the North Wales resort. The trip was declared feasible and plans were taking shape when Aberconwy Council withdrew as sponsors. Encouraged by initial responses, however, WSN decided to go ahead with the trip taking on the full financial responsibility.

Waverley *at Princes Landing Stage, Liverpool.*
Moored astern is the Isle of Man Steam Packet's Ben-My-Chree, *and the Mersey Ferry* Royal Iris *sails past.*

An expectant crowd greets Waverley *at Fleetwood on Sunday 8th May 1977.*

So, on Thursday 28th April 1977 *Waverley*, having revived the sailing from Campbeltown and Arran for the Ayr Agricultural Show earlier in the day, left Campbeltown just before midnight and turned south after clearing Davaar. *Waverley* reached Princes Landing Stage, Liverpool at 4.30pm on the Friday.

Llandudno Pier celebrations were launched when *Waverley* called at 2pm on 1st May with a full load from Liverpool. A cruise was then given to Amlwch. Public, school, pensioners and charter sailings were given on the Mersey that week. The excursion to Beaumaris on Saturday 7th May was cut short by heavy seas but the weather smiled on the Sunday trip to Fleetwood and Morecambe Bay. The following afternoon, *Waverley* sailed for Ayr.

Left: An engineer's view of the triple expansion steam engine. Above: Waverley in the far famed Kyles of Bute

A BLEAK DAY

But it all nearly came to an end on Friday 15th July 1977. *Waverley* was on her usual Friday sailing from Glasgow to Kilcreggan and Dunoon with a cruise to Loch Long and Loch Goil. Delays on the river in the morning, a tight schedule made even more so by adverse tides, an attempt to save precious minutes by swinging inside the Gantocks when approaching Dunoon from the north (it had worked easily on other occasions), the beginning of the ebb tide, a sluggish helm response, a list to port caused by people waiting to disembark; all combined to cause *Waverley* to bear down on one of the marker buoys off the Gantocks. Captain Neill took evasive action and rang down an emergency "Full Astern". The buoy was avoided but as the ship moved astern she caught on a pinnacle of Gantocks rock.

Waverley took water aft and the ebbing tide left her impaled. Passengers were quickly transferred to the ferry *Sound of Shuna* and landed at Dunoon Pier. Despite strenuous attempts to free herself *(above)* she remained stranded until the next high tide. At midnight, *Waverley* floated off and was berthed at Dunoon Quay where the damage was inspected. Major repairs in drydock were required and she was not back in service until Thursday 1st September, although the motor vessel *Queen of Scots (right)* was chartered to cover as much of *Waverley's* schedule as possible. The loss of revenue from the best part of the season nearly proved fatal but, once again, *Waverley* survived to sail another day.

WIDENING HORIZONS

Sandown, Isle of Wight

With the experience gained in the Mersey trip WSN planned increasingly ambitious programmes. In the spring of 1978, *Waverley* sailed round Land's End for a four week stint of cruising on the South Coast, Isle of Wight, Thames and Medway. An even longer spell down south was made in April and May of 1979 and included five days on the Bristol Channel. The effect on the steamer's economics was quite dramatic. In 1979, *Waverley* carried 230,000 passengers, nearly double the 1975 figure. Of these, 66,000 had sailed on her while outside Scottish waters.

Fleetwood was the first port of call on *Waverley's* 1980 trip south, an operation that included Liverpool, the South Coast, Thames and Medway, and the Bristol Channel. *Waverley's* first master and the commander of her illustrious predecessor, Captain John Cameron, joined Captain Neill for a commemorative cruise marking the fortieth anniversary of the Dunkirk evacuation.

Waverley sailed from Deal on 12th May first to Cap Gris Nez and then followed one of the convoy routes used by the assorted flotilla that worked the miracle of the evacuation. Captain Cameron cast a wreath on the sea as memories went back to the day an earlier *Waverley* and much of her human cargo were finally defeated by repeated air attacks.

Deal

ROUND BRITAIN CRUISE!

Waverley was to make history in 1981 when she became the first coastal steamer to sail round Britain offering excursions at various ports on her way round.

It is difficult to grasp the detailed planning that such a venture requires: fuel, pilotage, catering stores, local advertising, buses, ticket agents. A significant part of the shore office is taken over by Yellow Page telephone directories.

In April 1981, *Waverley*, complete with new boiler, made what was at that time her longest continuous voyage – Glasgow to Poole in Dorset – in 35 hours. The new boiler removed any need for expensive bunkering stops. It was two months before *Waverley* churned the waters of the Clyde again. The spring sailings were destined to encounter severe weather – wind, rain and even snow, but the people turned out regardless.

Scarborough.
Is this a record for cramming people on to a lighthouse's balcony?

An evening cruise on Friday 24th April from Poole and Bournemouth opened the "Steaming Round Britain" programme. A week later, *Waverley* was on the Medway for a couple of days before moving to London. Saturday 2nd May was a marathon. *Waverley* sailed from London's Tower Pier at 0700 to Cap Gris Nez, calling at Greenwich, Tilbury, Southend and Ramsgate. She returned to the capital at 0100 next morning – 18 hours steaming, with a full complement on the cross-Channel leg. Monday 4th was the May Day Holiday and *Waverley* gave a day trip from London to Gillingham on the Medway.

Worthing

The following day saw *Waverley's* final Thames cruise for 1981 and she then headed up the east coast. In the following weeks, excursions were given from Hull, Goole, New Holland, Newcastle, North and South Shields with calls at Scarborough and Middlesbrough. The final sailing in this part of the country was on Monday 25th May, the Spring Bank Holiday, when *Waverley* sailed from Newcastle, South and North Shields round the Farne Islands.

Right: City of Bridges - Waverley *manoeuvres in the River Tyne at Newcastle*

By the next evening, *Waverley* had sailed into the Firth of Forth and cruised from Granton (acting as Edinburgh's port) under the Bridges. *Waverley* had some busy days on the Forth especially on the sailings round the Bass Rock (30th May) and round the Isle of May and St. Andrews Bay (31st May).
Waverley left the Firth of Forth and set course for Duncansby Head, then through the infamous Pentland Firth and round Cape Wrath. Heading down the west coast a call was made at Kyle of Lochalsh and early on the morning of Thursday 4th June Oban Bay heard a paddle beat for the first time in nearly 40 years. The same day, passengers joined the paddler for the single trip to Ayr calling at Islay's Port Ellen. Her arrival at Ayr at 2200 completed her circuit of Great Britain.
Three days later she was off to the Bristol Channel, sailing down the east coast of Ireland to shelter from the strong westerly wind. Late on 22nd June, *Waverley* sailed from Penarth on her way back to Scotland.
The cruising schedule drawn up for *Waverley* in 1981 emphasises the change in fortune that has befallen the ship. What greater contrast can there be between *Waverley* in 1947 – a steamer that for her first years in service did not possess a passenger certificate allowing her beyond the Cumbrae Heads – and *Waverley* in 1981 – a steamer circumnavigating Britain? We also reflect that in 1973 she had been cast aside as having no further rôle to play in this country's tourist industry.
She undertook two more "Round Britain" marathons, clockwise in 1982 and anti-clockwise in 1983.

Capital bridges – Tower Bridge, London, opens up its arms for Waverley.

. . . while Edinburgh's Forth Railway Bridge and Waverley *provide examples of a great Scottish engineering heritage.*

WESTWARD HO!

Above: Waverley *and* Balmoral *at Ilfracombe.*

The Bristol Channel had long been a paddle steamer preserve. A summer charter on the Bristol Channel in 1887 had taken an earlier *Waverley* away from her Clyde duties. Her owners, Peter and Alec Campbell decided to transfer their activities to the area and the name of P. & A. Campbell became synonymous with the Channel steamers. The last paddler of the line, *Bristol Queen,* was withdrawn in August 1967 and thereafter motorships, latterly *Balmoral,* kept the Campbell flag flying until October 1980.

The 1947 *Waverley* brought the sound of paddles back to the Channel in May 1979 when the paddler had five successful days of cruising. The final sailing in 1979 was on Sunday 3rd June, when the paddler crossed from Penarth to Ilfracombe and continued on round Lundy Island, making an unscheduled stop to uplift about 60 people who had been stranded on the island.

Waverley *leaving the Victorian pier at Penarth on an evening charter sailing.*
She is carrying a full complement, and among the crowd of spectators on the pier are many who were unable to be aboard.

The elegant pier structure, which remains one of the most important pick-up points for Waverley *and* Balmoral, *celebrated its Centenary in 1994.*

Each spring before beginning the main Clyde programme, *Waverley* gives a short season of excursions on the Channel. Her schedule normally includes most of the traditional calling points, with Ilfracombe, famous for its Devon cream teas, still the favourite destination, while the island of Lundy, 12 miles from the Devon coast, receives regular visits.

The historic port of Bristol is approached by navigating the narrow twisting River Avon, with its notorious Horseshoe Bend and spectacular Gorge. *Waverley's* first visit to the city was in October 1986, and she has returned in subsequent years. Less common ports of call include Sharpness, Bideford, Tenby and Padstow:

Waverley's arrival at this Cornish resort in 1988 was the first by a paddle steamer for 21 years. On Saturday 27th May 1989 the paddler gave three special cruises from Clevedon to mark the re-opening of its Victorian pier.

The combined energy and resources of many individuals, backed by WSN expertise, rescued the motorship *Balmoral* from oblivion at Dundee and brought her to Glasgow for a major refit. In April 1986 *Balmoral* resumed her sailings on the Bristol Channel where she has continued to provide the main summer programme of cruises. Outwith this time she maintains an excursion schedule which rivals *Waverley's* in scope and ingenuity.

FROM PORTLAND BILL TO THE POOL OF LONDON

Paddle steamer sailings on the South Coast continued well into the 1960s. After a gap of a decade or so, *Waverley* revived this tradition and has maintained a presence in the area ever since. One of the most memorable days *Waverley* has spent on the South Coast was 17th September 1982 when the paddler was a floating grandstand for over 1000 people at the emotional return to Portsmouth of HMS *Invincible* after the Falklands Campaign.

While in the Southampton area, *Waverley* often meets up with passenger liners such as *Queen Elizebeth 2 (below)*. Encounters on a more modest scale are regularly scheduled with the steamship *Shieldhall*, the former Clyde sludge hopper now preserved as a passenger ship.

The commemoration in 1990 of the 50th Anniversary of the Dunkirk evacuation involved *Waverley* to an even greater extent than that of ten years previously. On Thursday 24th May she accompanied the "little ships" from Dover across the Channel and took part in a wreath-laying ceremony close to the French coast. Three days later she took her passengers, again from Dover, to the Beaches Remembrance Service off Dunkirk, and the weekend was rounded off on the Monday by her sailing from Ramsgate to meet the "little ships" returning.

Pre-war, Ramsgate was the destination of several London-based paddle steamers such as *Royal Sovereign* and *Royal Eagle*, and *Waverley* follows in their wake. Leaving from the Pool of London, she first passes under the raised arms of the 100-year-old Tower Bridge. This is in vivid contrast to the style of the Thames Flood Barrier which was built in the 1980s. A regular calling point for *Waverley* is the mile-and-a-quarter long Southend Pier – the longest in Britain. A highlight of every Thames visit is the "Parade of Steam" when *Waverley* meets up with her older "sister".

KINGSWEAR CASTLE

It was as long ago as 1967 that the Paddle Steamer Preservation Society purchased the small paddle steamer *Kingswear Castle*. She dates from 1924 and so is *Waverley's* senior by 23 years.

The 110' steamer is propelled by a compound diagonal engine built in 1904 and transferred to *Kingswear Castle* from an earlier paddler of the same name. This makes the engine one of the oldest marine engines to survive in Britain.

In 1924, the coal-fired *Kingswear Castle* joined a fleet of three small paddlers and two screw motorships on the picturesque one and a half hour trip between Totnes and Dartmouth on the River Dart – "The English Rhine" it has been called. Just as *Waverley* was to be the last paddler built for the Clyde, *Kingswear Castle* proved to be the last of her class constructed for the Dart. During the Second World War she was requisitioned and served as a tender at Dartmouth for both Royal and U.S. Navies.

Kingswear Castle's virtual sister, *Totnes Castle* was withdrawn after the 1963 season and *Kingswear Castle*, now the last surviving Dart paddler, was laid up at the end of the 1965 season and acquired by the PSPS in 1967 for restoration. Progress was slow but the success of *Waverley* gave the *Kingswear Castle* project a needed credibility and impetus. After years of work by volunteers, the paddler sailed under her own power again in November 1983 with *Waverley's* Captain David Neill in command. She was now far from the River Dart and it was the River Medway that frothed under her paddle beat.

During the 1984 summer a limited programme of sailings was offered from Strood Pier on the Medway. It was 1985 before a full passenger certificate was obtained for *Kingswear Castle* and a summer of sailings from the Medway piers and Southend was achieved.

A good memory was required to recall when two paddlers had last met in the Medway, but this was the setting for the first "official" meeting of the two steamers saved by the PSPS, *Waverley* and *Kingswear Castle,* on Sunday 16th September 1984. The former was on a day trip from London with the latter sailing from Strood. *Kingswear Castle,* still coal-fired, continues to offer a variety of cruises on the Medway from her base at Chatham Historic Dockyard, and sometimes ventures as far as Whitstable, Southend and the centre of London. Although it now happens almost annually, each rendezvous of Britain's only two operational paddle steamers still captures the imagination of PSPS members and public alike.

Opposite: Waverley *and* Kingswear Castle *steaming together in the Medway. A third steamer,* Medway Queen, *is seen in the background awaiting restoration.*

ACROSS THE IRISH SEA

Above: Waverley *at Youghal (County Cork). The Irish tricolour flies from the foremast, and a large crowd waits to board.*

In April of 1985, *Waverley* paid her first visit to a foreign country when several days were spent sailing from ports in Eire. During this time, the Irish tricolour was flown as a courtesy flag. Pursers, catering and souvenir shop staff faced the unprecedented hazards of pricing in Irish punts! She returned the following year sailing from, among other places, Dublin, Cork and Youghal.

Northern Ireland had to wait a further five years to welcome the last sea-going paddle steamer, a weekend of sailings being given from Belfast.

Waverley has taken day trippers to the Isle of Man from Scotland (Garlieston), Ulster (Donaghadee) and England (Whitehaven) and has also performed coastal cruises and sailings right round the island. Passengers on the first Garlieston sailing in 1985 received an unexpected bonus when their "day trip" became a weekend. The outward journey was lively, as shown by the photographs on the inside back cover, and continued bad weather precluded her return until 0600 on the Monday morning.

Below: Donaghadee.

TO THE ISLES

Waverley's first passenger sailings in Highland waters were a minor part of the "Steaming Round Britain" programme in 1981. For the next six years, around the May Day Holiday weekend, she gave a short season of cruises based on Oban and visiting such places as Fort William and Iona, with the first visit in fifty years by a paddler to the Sacred Isle being given on Saturday 24th April 1982. The 1988 Western Isles season was extended to include Mallaig, Kyle of Lochalsh and Portree, but this paled into insignificance when compared to the following year's developments.

The last time that a paddler had been seen in the Outer Hebrides was in October 1943 when *Pioneer* had called at Tarbert (Harris) on livestock sailings. Paddle steamer excursion sailings in this area were almost unheard of, so *Waverley's* 1989 visit to Lochmaddy, Tarbert and Stornoway was indeed a historic event.

Above: 8th May 1984: Congestion at Craignure, Isle of Mull. The ferry Glen Sannox *shares the pier with* Waverley *while Olsen's cruise liner* Black Prince *lies off awaiting the return of her passengers.*

Left: Waverley *at Castlebay on the island of Barra. On an islet in the bay is Kishmul Castle, ancestral home of the MacNeils of Barra.*

The final (so far!) extension of *Waverley's* Hebridean journeyings was in 1990, which saw her paddling to the southern islands of South Uist and Barra. Stuart Cameron, a long-standing member of *Waverley's* "Commodore Club", reminisces: "Just after noon, *Waverley* berthed at the pier at Lochboisdale for the first time. No one could remember the last time that a paddle steamer had called there and many South Uist folk were there to greet us. A special passenger disembarked. He was an octogenarian from Barra who had never left his native island before that day, and when he stepped off *Waverley's* gangway on to South Uist soil it was the only other part of the world that he had ever stood upon! *Waverley* has a knack of encouraging folk to break old habits."

Left: Portree, Isle of Skye, on a Sunday morning in May 1989.

Facing page above: Waverley's *historic visit to Otter Ferry on Easter Sunday 1993.*

below: Although the pier at the village of Arrochar was closed in 1972, and almost nothing of it remains, there is a substantial pier at the former Torpedo Testing Station on the west bank of the loch. This has allowed Waverley *to return to the sailing for which she was built.*
This view shows her making a visit on Easter Sunday, 1996.

HOME WATERS

unexpected. On the last Sunday in September 1992 *Waverley* became the first steamer since March 1940 to call at the tiny fishing village of Carradale. Amazingly, her arrival was captured on film by a photographer who, as a boy, had witnessed the previous call 52 years earlier!

The following Easter another innovation devised by Captain Michel brought out the public in their hundreds. Otter Ferry Pier, last used by a passenger steamer in 1914, was found to be in surprisingly good condition and permission for *Waverley* to call was generously given by the owners. At 1440 on Easter Sunday, Captain Michel gently brought the steamer alongside, to the delight of the crowds of sightseers on the shore.

Over 400 passengers streamed ashore, disturbing the tranquillity of Loch Fyne with their clicking camera shutters. It was an emotional farewell as *Waverley* left for home, giving the traditional three long blasts on her steam whistle.

Waverley still spends her main season from late June until the end of August at home on the Clyde. Her innovative programme of 1975 has gradually evolved but the essential features continue. Families can still sail from the heart of Glasgow to the traditional resorts of Dunoon, Rothesay and Millport. The breathtaking passage through the Kyles of Bute never fails to make a lasting impression on the tourist, while the crossings to Brodick and Campbeltown provide a real "deep sea" experience.

Clyde cruising is enlivened by occasional trips to unusual destinations such as Inveraray, Stranraer and round Ailsa Craig. The Clyde can still produce the

A LEGEND REBORN

By the mid 1990s, continually escalating maintenance costs and new marine safety requirements were threatening *Waverley's* long term future. Plans were drawn up which would allow the vessel to be rebuilt to an 'as new' condition, restoring much of her original character but, at the same time, incorporating modern safety equipment. The Heritage Lottery Fund awarded a grant of £2·7 million and significant funding was also provided by PSPS, the European Regional Development Fund and various local councils and Enterprise Companies in the west of Scotland.

Tenders were received from five ship repair yards throughout the UK, with George Prior Engineering of Great Yarmouth being awarded the contract in late November 1999. The next eight months were to be the most dramatic in *Waverley's* 53 year history.

Just before Christmas 1999 she arrived at Prior's yard to be "rebuilt". Within a few days many of the ship's fittings had been stripped out. The replacement furniture and upholstery would be a faithful reproduction of the original designs.

In early February, 2000, she moved to a drydock across the River Yare. This was the narrowest drydock she had ever been in – she could only get in after her paddleboxes and sponsons had been removed.

Below: With her funnels and sponsons removed, Waverley *is assisted into drydock*

During January, the ship's huge triple expansion engine was dismantled and lifted ashore for renovation. Although the major components were renovated in Great Yarmouth, many smaller items were treated elsewhere. Refurbishment of various pumps, for example, was carried out by *Waverley's* own engineers at the workshops in Glasgow, while other pieces of equipment were sub-contracted to specialist firms.

By mid-summer the various components were brought together at Great Yarmouth, and re-assembly began.

Below: The massive 8-ton crankshaft receives some last-minute attention before being lifted back aboard.

The hull and superstructure were extensively shotblasted, inside and outside. Replacement of corroded steel plates was extensive, as can be seen in this view of the boiler room *(above)*, but, perhaps surprisingly, much of the original 1947 plating was found to be fit for further service and has been retained.

The new paddleboxes and sponsons were prefabricated in George Prior's works in Hull, taken by road to Great Yarmouth and lifted into position by crane.

Below: Fitting the forward starboard sponson – this is now the Gents' toilet.

Right: An aerial view taken in mid May highlights the extent of the rebuild in progress.
Three of the four new sponsons are in position, a tarpaulin covers the empty boiler room, and part of the promenade deck is being plated in steel. Later, a wooden deck will be laid on top and the new after deckhouse fitted.
To comply with modern safety regulations a new escape stairway from the Dining Saloon was required. The opening for this is clearly visible.

Above: The arrival of the first of the two new boilers designed and manufactured by Cochran Boilers of Annan.

Left: One of the paddle-wheels on the quayside after overhaul. The two lowest floats have not yet been replaced to prevent the wheel from turning in the River Yare's six knot current during the fitting operation

Right: The refurbished starboard paddlewheel is lowered into position.

Left: The 'new' Waverley *takes shape.*

Below, left: New aluminium funnels and deckshelter are in position. Hull painting is in progress but the wood graining effect has still to be applied to the deckshelter.

Below: Waverley *steams away from Great Yarmouth on trials on Saturday 12th August.*